Text and photography: Alexandra Arellanc
(Professor of the Instituto de Investigación,
Facultad de Turismo y Hotelería, Universidad de San Martín de Porres, Lima-Perú)
Photography and coordination: Neus Escandell-Tur
Photographic collaboration: Fototeca Stone (page: 4),
César Vivanco (pages: 75, 76 and 77-f. 1),
Marta Esteban (pages: 48-f. 2; 52-f. 2; 59-f. 2;
63-f. 2; 64; 74-f. 3; 82-f. 1) and
Roberto Bensi (pages: 62-f. 3; 79),
Collaboration in publication: Alejandra Rojas
(Instituto de Investigación,
Facultad de Turismo y Hotelería, Universidad de San Martín de Porres)
Cartography: Eduard Busquets
Translation: Lillian Valdés
Original title: Todo Cuzco
Sponsor: Instituto de Investigación,
Facultad de Turismo y Hotelería, Universidad de San Martín de Porres
Printing: Fisa-Escudo de Oro (Barcelona-Spain).
Publication: Centro de Estudios Regionales Andinos
«Bartolomé de las Casas» (Cuzco-Perú).
Copyright: Centro de Estudios Regionales Andinos
«Bartolomé de las Casas» (Cuzco-Perú),
and Instituto de Investigación,
Facultad de Turismo y Hotelería, Universidad de San Martín de Porres.

Distributor: Centro de Estudios Regionales Andinos
«Bartolomé de las Casas»
Address: Carlos Alayza y Roel 2626
Lince, Apartado 14087
Lima 14-PERU
Tel: (511) 442-9992 and 441-9610
Fax: (511) 442-7894
E-Mail: Postmaster@cbclim.inv.pe

cbc

I.S.B.N. 84-8387-055-X

Dep. Legal B. 26383

Acknowledgements

First of all, we would like to express our appreciation to Michel Van Aerde, Beatriz Garland, Juan Carlos García and Henrique Urbano, of the Centro Bartolomé de las Casas, as well as Johan Leuridan Huys, dean of the Faculty of Tourism of the University of San Martín de Porres, for their support in the publication of ALL CUZCO. The preparation of ALL CUZCO is the result of several visits to the city and the valley of Cuzco between 1987-1991 and from July-October 1996. There were many people who accompanied us on all of the routes mentioned in this text and who provided their suggestions for the preparation of the guide which we are presenting today. Special mention must be made of Gerardo Fernández, Isabel Iriarte, and Antonio Acosta, for all of the patience they demonstrated in the extended visits to the Cuzco Valley which we subjected them to for several days. D. Federico Letona helped us in all those questions related to Colonial Art; the Jesuit Father José R. González Ecija, Pablo Bustamante, Moisés Cerí Morales, and the director of the Casa Garcilaso, kindly allowed us to photograph the paintings in the churches of Andahuaylillas, San Juan de Huaro and Pucyura, as well as in Casa Garcilaso, respectively. Father Bernard Fulcrand and the photographer César Vivanco provided us with advice on the overall preparation of the guide. Nevertheless, all possible errors are our sole responsibility. Finally, we would like to express our appreciation to all of the members of the Centro Bartolomé de las Casas for all of the attention they provided during our stay in Cuzco.

Alexandra Arellano and Neus Escandell-Tur

Prologue

ALL CUZCO offers an accurate, reliable guide which includes new information for the traveller who wants to become familiar with the city of Cuzco and the surrounding area. The detailed research on the archaeological and colonial areas, the combination of Andean scenery and colonial art, the plentiful photographs and well-documented historical explanation make this guide an essential travelling companion for those who wish to become familiar with the ancient capital of the Incas.

ALL CUZCO is a guide which is different from those one often finds displayed in travel agencies. It provides the traveller with information on the rich and varied artistic wealth of this area, opening the reader's eyes to the splendor of the snowy peaks of the Andes or the gorges which lead down to the hot Amazon region. The itineraries chosen shall take the traveller on unusual but safe routes, and shall help him or her to understand the secrets hidden in the Incan rocks, the pre-Hispanic walls and homes, the colonial churches and chapels.

ALL CUZCO is an extensive guide. Although it is true that the city and the region are known for the extraordinary ancient fortress city of Machu Picchu, one must not forget that the wealth of Cuzco is more than this precious jewel of nature and of Andean history. The guide describes the wide variety existing in the Andean areas and in the cultures which have developed throughout several millenniums.

For all of these reasons, the Faculty of Tourism of the University of San Martín de Porres is proud to have participated, in collaboration with the Centro Bartolomé de las Casas, in the research, production and publication of this guide. We hope that this model and the product it creates serve as an example for future publications. The enriching experience of the publication of ALL CUZCO could lead to a new collection of guides on Peru. In fact, with the infinite variety of climates and the generosity of its people, the Andes deserve nothing less.

Dr. Johan Leuridan Huys
Dean of the Faculty of Tourism
University of San Martín De Porres
Lima-Peru

Night view of the Plaza de Armas, in Cuzco.

Pre-Hispanic Cuzco

The mythical origins of Cuzco

In approximately the fifteenth century, a town of uncertain origins appeared in the Cuzco Valley. Some say that its inhabitants came from Lake Titicaca. Others state that they came out of the caves or niches located in a town called Pacaritambo, not far from the city. Its inhabitants called themselves the «Children of the Sun»: they were the Incas. Little is known about what the city was like before the arrival of these mysterious people. The Indians -the Huayllas, the Sauseros, the Ayarmacas-lived in several scattered towns. There is even talk of a chief, Alcaviza. Whatever the case, according to the ancient legends, the Incas established alliances with the people who lived in the valley and their mythical chiefs, the four Ayar siblings, established firm friendships with the ancient settlers. As of this point, the story of the Cuzco valley is united with that of the Ayar siblings and their descendants, the Incas.

Calle Hatunrumiyoq, pedestrian walkway where the Stone with 12 Angles is located.

The Cuzco valley and its setting

In the center of this vast valley with hills facing towards the south, the town of Cuzco began. Its boundaries were formed by the Huatanay River. To the east, the hills separated Cuzco from the Yucay Valley where the Vilcanota River grows wider. The pampas were rich and productive, and the small lakes which irrigated the region guaranteed the survival of the towns: in the high areas, potatoes were grown, and in the valleys, corn was the main crop. Throughout the valley, herds of *llamas* and *alpacas* provided meat and woolw for the inhabitants of the area. Not far away the vast jungle area was located and, on the ridge of the mountain, the coveted coca leaves grew.

The arrival of new masters changed the lifestyle of those living in the area. The Incas not only came in order to settle and grow crops on the rich lands of the valley. With time, it became evident that they had other motives as well. They were fearless conquerors, and the entire valley was easy prey for their power. Nevertheless, there were also other powerful peoples in the distance who at some time would confront the warlike plans of the masters of the Cuzco Valley.

The Incas and the Chancas

The real test came in the mid-fifteenth century, when

Stone with 12 Angles, in the wall of the Palace of Inca Roca.

Viracocha Inca was the leader and chief of the Incas. For reasons which are not clear, a warlike and conquering people reached the foot of the hills, and panic spread among the leaders of the valley. Viracocha feared the invaders, and delegated the decision regarding the fate of the towns of the valley to his sons. It was his offspring Pachacuti Inca who would achieve the victory over the enemy, the Chancas. After this triumph, the valleys and pampas of Cuzco, its punas and peaks, would remain

Calle Loreto or Intik'ijllu.

Calle Hatunrumiyoq, next to the Archbishopric where the Museum of Religious Art is located.

area. They were sent to collect the gold needed to ensure the rescue of Atawallpa, who had been taken prisoner in Cajamarca in 1532.

Pachacuti Inca demanded that his father recognize his military merits without denying the respect due to the elderly. But Viracocha Inca, humiliated by the frivolity of his favorite son Inca Urcon, abandoned Cuzco forever and sought refuge in the nearby lands of the pampas which, towards the northeast, lead towards Pisac and the Yucay Valley.

Pachacuti Inca, organizer of the city

As absolute ruler of the region, Pachacuti Inca constructed the city and planned its neighborhoods and boundaries. In the north, the ill-named Fortress or Sacsayhuaman, with its monumental walls, projects from the hills of carved stone and the archaeological ruins where the ancient masters of the valley celebrated their rituals. The symbols remind one of the importance of water. Irrigation channels pass through here or can be seen from here. The waters descended to the terraced gardens of the city and irrigated the lands where crops were grown further south, on the hills where presently San Sebastián and San Jeró-nimo are located. Pachacuti Inca considered the Sacsayhuaman the head of the city, which ended in what was referred to as the «Puma Tail» or Pumachupan, where the Huatanay River begins. Both of these points, located at opposite ends, defined the two main areas of the city: the upper area, or *hanan*, and the lower region, or *hurin*. Between these two points, in the center of the city, the main square, Huacaypata Plaza, was built. The plaza was an area of ritual importance where the ceremonies which marked the religious life of the Incas were performed. The most sacred area of the plaza was the *usno*, a ceremonial altar made of stone covered with gold. On this altar, the blood from the sacrifices and the sacred chicha were strewn. A crack along the length of the altar enabled the blood and chicha to enter the underground channels which, like veins, nurture the sacred area of the Temple of the Sun or Coricancha.

The Acllawasi or «House of the Virgins of the Sun», with its walls of finely carved stone, was located near the plaza. In the seventeenth century, part of this structure was donated to the Convent of Santa Catalina, occupied at present by nuns from the religious order with the same name. Nearby one can see the Church of the Company of Jesus, which occupied the former stately home of the conquistador Hernando Pizarro. This structure was originally the Amaru Cancha of the Incas, the area where they kept their animals, especially those which represented the rich and varied fauna of the Amazon. It was, one could say, a sort of zoological garden. In the front of the square, on the other side of the *usno*, other important buildings were also built, which ended on the corner where the Saphi stream comes down.

Continuing along the valley upriver, against the current, one could find a sacred bush with the same name as the stream, saphi: the mythical origins of the city were also attributed to this stream. In this area, presently occupied by the Santa Ana neighborhood, the Spanish conquistadors entered the city for the first time, crossing the muddy stream on horseback and continuing towards the Temple of the Sun.

The Temple of the Sun or Coricancha

Within the walls of the Temple of the Sun, there was a significant amount of gold. The ritual objects and other instruments which were not confiscated by Spanish greed were also made of gold. The temple was located on a hill towards the southeast, quite distant from Huacaypata Plaza. The temple gardens extended down to what is presently known as the Avenida del Sol, where the underground waters from the Saphi valley run down towards Pumachupan. The walls which defined the sacred area, some of which were employed in the construction of the Church of Santo Domingo after the Spanish invasion, have been well-conserved. The most impressive part is the wall which forms the base of the main altar of the present church, also serving as a window which looks out towards the west and the surrounding hills. The water channelled from the hills and fountains of the city, as well as the blood and sacred chicha from the sacrifices, reached the courtyards of this sacred area occupied by the Incas and their environment.

Huanacauri or the Sacred Hill of the Incas

Further south, near what is presently the airport, the most sacred hill of the Incas, Huanacauri, was located. Although it has been neglected, its memory is worth conserving. The entire ritual life of the Incas recalls the deeds which

Incan ceremonial vessel found in a tomb in 1957, Archaeological Museum of Cuzco.

occurred in these hills where, according to legend, the mythical Ayar brothers and sisters first entered the valley of Cuzco. This area provided a sacred view point for the entire valley. Perhaps for this reason the ancestors of the Incas honored these hills with their memory and their descendants included them in the ritual life of the city. Huanacauri was a strategic location. From the peak, which legend associates with the figure of Ayar Uchu, one of the mythical ancestors of the Incas, one can see the hills surrounding the city and the lands where the Huatanay River flows southward. The town of San Sebastián, referred to in prehistoric times as Sañu, is not far from here. The name is related to pottery activities, since there is a good amount of clay in this region, and the Incas knew how to make good use of it. Opposite Huanacauri, towards the south, we find the peaks of Pachatusan. There are archaeological ruins in this area which confirm its importance. These high ridges act as the physical limit of the city of Cuzco, and in pre-Hispanic times they were the border which defined the ritual area of the Incas. Beyond, the scenery extends towards Vilcanota Valley and the sharp descent of the peaks which lead down towards the Sacred Valley. In fact, the border of the city was the Yucay Valley itself, where some Incan rituals were performed, thus confirming that this area of the river was also sacred land.

The Four Roads or Tawantinsuyu

The years in which Pachacuti Inca held the political power are also important because of Incan expansion beyond the borders of the outlying areas near Cuzco during this period. There are several archaeological findings which demonstrate that the power of the Incas extended in several directions during these years. Although there is no clear documental evidence regarding the extent of the conquests of Pachacuti Inca, there is no doubt that towards the end of the fifteenth century the Incas had reached the north of Chile and the northwest of Argentina as well as several coastal regions in the west. In the northern region, Pachacuti Inca's successors such as Tupac Yupanqui and Huayna Capac travelled as far as Tumebamba, in Ecuador, and established their political and military dominion in these areas.

The dominion of the vast territory of the Andes is reflected in the expression Tawantinsuyu or «The Four Roads». Modern authors speak of the Tawantinsuyu Empire. The

suyus or roads divided the Andes in four directions: to the north, the chinchaysuyu; to the south, the collasuyu; to the east, the antisuyu and to the west, the continsuyu.

Incan idol and gold llama which served as offering (5 centimeters), Archaeological Museum of Cuzco.

Pre-Hispanic Quero, Archaeological Museum of Cuzco.

Panacas and curacas

The Incas could not maintain power in such a vast area without a socio-political and military organization. Since the mythical times of the Ayar siblings, he Incas always displayed an unwavering desire to occupy a broad region of the Andean territory. After settling in the region near Cuzco and dominating the people residing in this area, they gradually began to extend their power until they occupied the entire valley, and beyond the valley, much of the Andes. Without a strong, disciplined military strength and the ability to unite the people and integrate them within the Incan empire, it would not have been possible to successfully occupy and establish control in these regions. For this reason, the Incas developed forms of political power which were concentrated in large groups of families or *ayllus*. The governing groups were called *panacas*. It is uncertain how many of these existed, but when the Spaniards arrived at least ten *panacas* were recognized. The members of each panaca were joined by ties of blood, and these men were responsible for the Incan political and religious power. The Inca was the figure who represented all of the *panacas*. On the local level, the Incas conserved the existing traditional authorities and used them to wield and to spread their own political power. These local authorities were called *curacas*. They were in charge of a rather large group of families, or *ayllus*. Some were powerful because of the wealth of the region within their territory. Others, in more isolated areas, lived in very uncertain conditions. The Incas knew how to gain the The the *curacas* by offering them aid during periods of hunger or scarcity. The Incas usually established alliances with

Typical view of the citadel of Machu Picchu.

the most powerful local authorities, and traded goods and services with them.

Incan gods and heroes

The Incas worshipped the Sun, or *Inti*, as master of all things. They also worshipped the Moon, or *Quilla*, as well as some stars. Likewise, the Thunder and Lightning formed part of their worship, and they also felt a general sense of devotion for the hills and peaks. The important liturgical ceremonies were held in the hills, and some of these were especially chosen for the rites of the *panacas*. There was also great devotion for the Mother Earth or *Pachamama*. As of the sixteenth century, as a result of the influence of Catholicism, they also spoke of the god Viracocha as the supreme god of the Incas. The name Viracocha came to designate the Spaniards, who were considered representatives of this supreme god.

The mummies of the ancestors played an extremely important role in Incan ceremonies. The niches in the walls were used to display these mummies, which were carried in processions during the group political and religious activities, in the city as well as in other areas.

Incan rituals and liturgical celebrations

There were three main periods of the year in which the Incas celebrated important rituals. The first of these was *Inti Raymi*, an agricultural feast usually held in April or May. During this celebration, the people expressed their appreciation to the Sun and other gods for the crops and the increase in livestock. The second important period was referred to as *Coya Raymi*. This period took place in September, with the coming of the first rain, and included rituals meant to protect the towns and the governing groups from all evils. *Capac Raymi*, which was celebrated in December, was the third period of importance for the celebration of rituals. These were liturgical celebrations of a more political nature during which the youths who would later form the military and political elite were chosen.

Tourists on Huayna Picchu peak, Machu Picchu.

The Tower or Temple of the Sun, Machu Picchu. One of the windows is perfectly aligned with the point of dawn on the solstice, 21st June.

Machu Picchu

The physical surroundings of the citadel

All of the tourist activities carried out in Peru are centered around Machu Picchu. Over time this area has gradually become the symbol of pre-Hispanic life and the splendor of the Andes. Its geographical location and physical setting make Machu Picchu a dream-like place with an exceptional beauty comparable to the most beautiful scenery created by nature and embellished by the hand of man. The deep and turbulent waters of the Vilcanota River, which runs through the Sacred Valley, meanders at its feet. Not far from here the imposing peaks of Nevado Salkantay rise above 6,000 metres. This setting makes Machu Picchu more than simply scenery. With the peak of Huayna Picchu and its marvelous jungle areas nearby, this is an awe-inspiring location which conserves a mysterious and sacred air.

The exact time when the pre-Hispanic buildings were constructed is not known with certainty. The most recent research states that the first buildings can be attributed to Inca Pachacuti, the well-known organizer of Cuzco, who was also active in this region. The architectural structures reflect the most classic Incan style, with walls of carved stone, typical trapezoidal doors, terraced gardens and the ever-present *Intihuatana* or stone «which moors the sun» and orients man in time, marking the seasons and the hours.

The modern rediscovery of the citadel

The contemporary history of Machu Picchu begins with the expedition undertaken by the American archaeologist Hiram Bingham in 1911. Bingham, who was attracted by the Andean scenery and by curiosity, wanted to explore the Amazon and the Andean regions. When he found these buildings, he thought he had come across what was referred to as Vilcabamba, area which historically had served as the «final refuge of the Incas» fleeing from the Spanish conquistadors. He failed to identify the name and the location correctly: Machu Picchu was not Vilcabamba. Nevertheless, the writings and the work contributed by Bingham's expedition had a permanent effect on the region, providing a symbol for Peru and for humanity. Many of the names attributed to the areas and the buildings are a result of this expedition. Some of these names are realistic; others are imaginary denominations.

View of Machu Picchu.

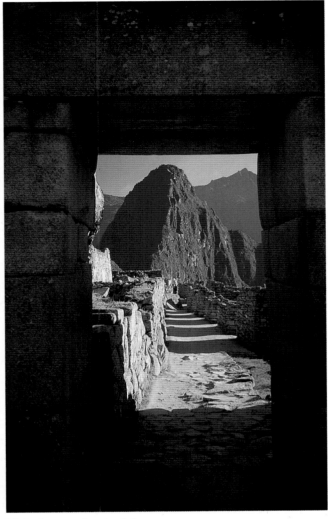

Main door to the citadel.

Organization of the Machu Picchu area

The buildings are distributed within the citadel area in a manner similar to that found in other Incan archaeological ruins. The names designated are modern or hypothetical. They speak of several sectors, some of which are easily understood. The sector set aside for growing is evident because of the presence of terraces, irrigated by the water which comes out of a carved stone fountain. There is a building which includes many niches, where the mummies of the ancestors or deceased were placed: this seems to merit the name of Temple of the Sun. These niches or openings in the walls are characteristic of the classic Incan constructions. A cavern suggests the existence of a royal tomb or the burial place of a leader of great political and administrative importance. Around this tomb, there are structures with finely carved shapes which seem to suggest an area set aside for the royalty: the most important area of the citadel.

The sector referred to as the «Temple of the Three Windows» (*templo de las tres ventanas*) is, along with aforementioned area for the royalty, one of the most important structures. The stones or rocks on which these constructions have been built display a notable architectural harmony which provides these megalithic stones with a sense of sacredness. The three windows

Archaeological ruins of Machu Picchu. View of Huayna Picchu from the agricultural sector.

Terraced gardens in Machu Picchu.

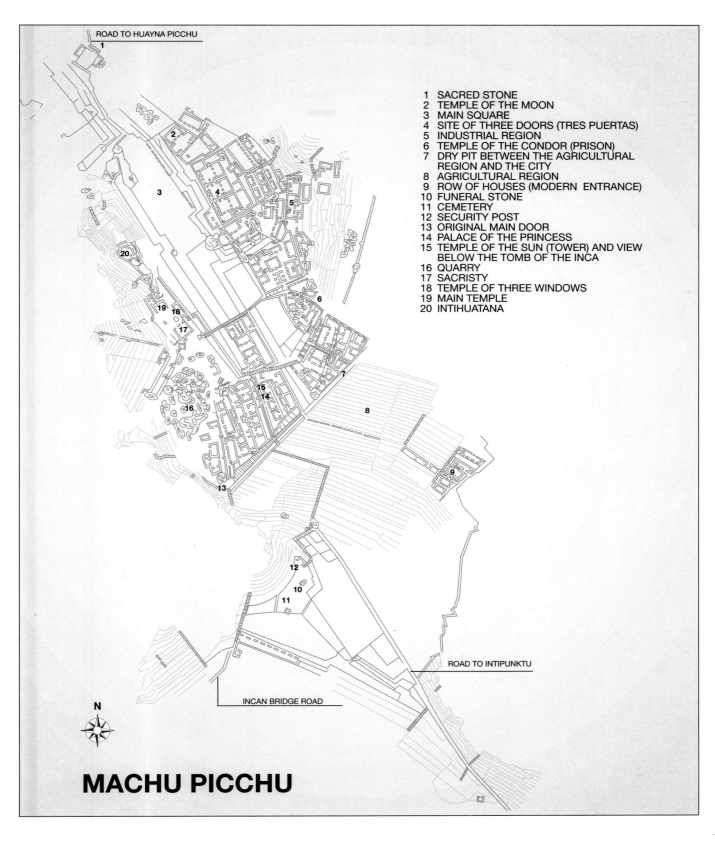

ROAD TO HUAYNA PICCHU

1 SACRED STONE
2 TEMPLE OF THE MOON
3 MAIN SQUARE
4 SITE OF THREE DOORS (TRES PUERTAS)
5 INDUSTRIAL REGION
6 TEMPLE OF THE CONDOR (PRISON)
7 DRY PIT BETWEEN THE AGRICULTURAL
   REGION AND THE CITY
8 AGRICULTURAL REGION
9 ROW OF HOUSES (MODERN ENTRANCE)
10 FUNERAL STONE
11 CEMETERY
12 SECURITY POST
13 ORIGINAL MAIN DOOR
14 PALACE OF THE PRINCESS
15 TEMPLE OF THE SUN (TOWER) AND VIEW
   BELOW THE TOMB OF THE INCA
16 QUARRY
17 SACRISTY
18 TEMPLE OF THREE WINDOWS
19 MAIN TEMPLE
20 INTIHUATANA

ROAD TO INTIPUNKTU

INCAN BRIDGE ROAD

N

MACHU PICCHU

View of Machu Picchu with the «Hiram Bingham» road from Huayna Picchu.

Machu Picchu.

Temple of the Three Windows, Machu Picchu.

remind one of the three windows of Pacaritambo, mentioned in the legends on the origin of the Incas. Near this temple there is another structure referred to as the main temple, with three walls and massive foundations, as well as a construction called the «sacristy».

Crossing the green area with our back to the main entrance, we reach the most ordinary section with the most neglected appearance. Here the structures no longer display the perfection of the «sector of the royalty», although in some of them there are still stones with unusual shapes which draw one's attention. Two of these are referred to as «mortars» since, according to some sources, they were used to grind the corn, although they seem to be too large for this purpose. Other buildings near the citadel face areas where crops were grown or which seem to have been used for rituals. One of the most noteworthy of these is the Temple of the Moon, with its fine architecture, located along the narrow path which leads to Huayna Picchu hill and surrounded by impressive terraces.

Machu Picchu and the Amazon area

The roads which lead from Machu Picchu to the jungle are difficult to follow, but access is not restricted. In this area, there is an extremely wide variety of species of flora and fauna and many examples of new scenery. To follow the routes along the lower ridge of the mountain, adjacent to the dense jungle, one should be in good physical condition because the heat naturally makes one tired. There are places where one can stop along the road and rest.

In Aguas Calientes it is not difficult to find lodging. One may also stay in the Machu Picchu Hotel, located within the citadel itself, although at present the latter has a limited capacity. As for food, there are sufficient supplies. One can remain in the region for several days and explore the exceptional routes along the ridge of the mountain and the jungle.

The Sacred Valley of the Incas
(See Route 2)

The borders of the Sacred Valley of the Incas

Continuing along the route which leads to Pisac, one reaches the Yucay Valley, generic name for a long, narrow valley which, in the southern region, goes back up to Urcos and towards the north, crossing Ollantaytambo before it finally reaches the citadel of Machu Picchu. Pisac is approximately 32 kilometers from the city of Cuzco. The entire valley extends along the Vilcanota River, and the waters of this river become more and more plentiful near the steep hills from which the melted snow flows down to the valley below. The climate is mild and the scenery is of a shade of green which, especially in the rainy period between November and April, is more pronounced than in the city of Cuzco. The area of the valley between Pisac and Ollantaytambo is known as the Sacred Valley of the Incas. Over the years, the power of the Incas became more and more firmly implanted. When the Spaniards arrived in this region, many activities were performed here, including architectural as well as agricultural pursuits. The terraces are a testimony of the vast production of food, and the Ollantaytambo ruins reflect the ambitious plans of the leaders of Cuzco.

Travelling through the archaeological ruins suggested in Route 2 of the Appendix, one may easily reach the conclusion that this entire region includes a vast wealth of ancient relics, comparable to the finest expressions of Incan art and the activities these reflect.

Pisac and its citadel

In the peaks in the Pisac area, which is a key point in the valley extending upriver towards Urcos, a splendid series of Incan monuments can be found, distributed in harmonious groups or «neighborhoods». In these areas there are traditional walls of carved stone, large homes (*casonas*) and ritual buildings, with a complex structure of terraces and irrigation channels which protect the area as though it were a fortress. One can follow the route by car or, better yet, walk along the path which crosses the terraced gardens. The beauty of the scenery is spectacular, making one easily forget the weariness caused by the walk or the soroche which the abrupt ascent brings about.

The Temple of the Sun, the Temple of the Moon and the carved stone referred to as *Intihuatana* express evident astronomical concerns. The area reserved for what could be called storehouses or granaries demonstrate the importance the Incas granted to the conservation of the crops.

Archaeological ruins in Pisac.

View of the Sacred Valley of the Incas from the Taray viewpoint.

Pisac.

Archaeological ruins in Ollantaytambo.

From Pisac to Urubamba

From Pisac, following the Vilcanota River towards the west, the narrow route between the river and the hills passes through the towns of Calca, Yucay and Urubamba before arriving at Ollantaytambo. Each of these towns also has a particular appeal. Many visitors come to these towns each year to witness the celebration of the feast days of the patron saints. In this area one can also find archaeological ruins which are not as well-known because one most travel along roads which are rarely used in order to reach them. For example, from Calca or Yucay one can reach the Huchuy Cuzco ruins, a well-conserved series of ruins of extraordinary archaeological beauty located in a mountainous area. Yucay is associated with some important events in Incan and colonial history. In the spacious Plaza de Armas we find a beautiful, impressive tree, the *pisonay*, whose leafy branches and beautiful flowers grant the town an air of festivity and elegance. The ruins of the Palace of the Inca Huayna Capac can also be found in this area. Huayna Capac died in the distant lands of Quito as a result of an unusual illness possibly caused by the bacteriological differences between the Europeans and the people of the North Andes. He was the father of Huascar and Atawallpa, brothers confronted in a battle for power when the Spanish army suddenly gained power in northern Peru. His remains reached Cuzco shortly after his death, and he was widely mourned by the people of Cuzco and the towns of the Sacred Valley he had so improved and loved.

Urubamba is not located far from here. Like Yucay, it has many restaurants and pleasant dining areas with reasonable prices. The nearby white mountain range provides the area with scenery of extraordinary beauty. The town offers the visitor a wide range of possibilities for rest and lodging, and includes a number of hotels and other lodging houses.

Ollantaytambo: The unfinished citadel of the Incas

The town of Ollantaytambo is located on the opposite end of the Pisac Valley. Here, the present town has maintained the pre-Hispanic plan. This second example of a noteworthy architectural site in the Sacred Valley is also of interest due to the size, style and originality of its buildings. This was one of the last areas in which construction was performed by the Incas before the arrival of the Spaniards. Many of the buildings begun in pre-Hispanic times were left unfinished. The abandoned stones and unfinished walls remain as testimonies of the battle in which Manco Capac faced the Spanish conquistadors. Overcome by the invaders, the Incas fled to the Vilcabamba jungle, area which served as a final refuge for what remained of the political legacy of the Incas.

Chinchero

After Maras, continuing along the road which returns to the city of Cuzco, we reach the town of Chinchero, located between Urubamba and Cuzco. This area is well-

Tower of the Church of Chinchero.

known for its ruins and for the lovely church where one can find many paintings from the Cuzco school. It is also an appropriate region to view the splendid snowcapped peaks in the surrounding area. Its history includes an exceptional figure: the cacique Don Mateo Pumacahua, adversary of another famous cacique, José Gabriel Condorcanqui, also known as Tupac Amaru II, leader of the major anti-colonial uprising in 1780. Pumacahua roused the Indians of the Cuzco region and defended the city of Cuzco from the rebel troops with their support. The exploits of Pumacahua played a decisive role in the destiny of the city of Cuzco, and the paintings conserved in the church call to mind these historical events and deeds. The church also houses other works of art and mural paintings by Diego Cusi Guamán, as well as several canvases by other artists. The main altarpiece is from the seventeenth century and represents the Virgin of Montserrat, to whom the church is dedicated.

Maras salt flats and the circular ruins in Moray

From Urubamba, crossing the bridge over the Vilcanota River, the road continues up the mountain and follows a winding route which leads to the towns on the pampas located on the northwestern side before entering the city of Cuzco. Maras, from which one can reach the salt flats and the Moray ruins, is not far from here.
The salt flats display a spectacle of unusual beauty. Located on a wide open hill above the Urubamba Valley, the salt water runs along channels which extend through the flooded lands and follow a more or less rectangular pattern, depending on the variations in the land. The water, which is exposed to the sun, leaves salt on the bed. Viewed from the peak, the myriad of rectangles look like an enormous painting designed by nature.
Inland, not far from Maras, one can find the Moray ruins. Here the terraces arranged in concentric circles and spread out at intervals from the lower to the upper region, are reminiscent of a Greek theater. For this reason, it is not clear exactly what role they played. The structure of these terraces seems to suggest agricultural activity which employed the air circulation within the circular area and the advantages offered by this type of construction for employing rain water as well as water from nearby regions.

Maras salt flats.

Maras salt flats. In the background, Urubamba. ▷

Pre-Hispanic towns in the Cuzco Valley

Pikillaqta, the pre-Incan area in the Cuzco Valley

Approximately 30 kilometers from Cuzco, continuing along the road to Urcos, there is a large archaeological site not far from the small lake at Huacarpay and the town of Lucre. Pikillaqta has its own particular characteristics. The Wari culture, which migrated from the present region of Ayacucho to southern Peru in approximately the sixth century A.D., once lived in this area. During the tenth and eleventh centuries, these people began to influence the towns located near Lake Titicaca. Over time, the Wari and the Tiawanaco became allies. It is clear that the Wari also settled further south.
Pikillaqta represents the limit of Wari expansion in the Cuzco Valley. Different types of buildings and the distribution of the inhabitants by well-defined neighborhoods and sectors can be found in the ruins. The walls, which in some cases reach up to 10 meters, are especially noteworthy. The areas set aside as storehouses, where the crops were kept, are also significant. There are also irrigation channels which transported the water for the crops from Lucre. The building methods and agricultural work influenced the Incas over time, but their sudden appearance in the region of the Cuzco Valley came about at the same time as a decrease in the Wari influence.

Huacarpay Lake, opposite Pikillaqta.

◁ *Partial view of the archaeological ruins in Moray.*

Tipón

Far from the route which leads from Cuzco to Urcos, nearly hidden in a valley which faces the town of Oropesa, we find the Incan ruins of Tipón. This is an outstanding archaeological site which includes the typical channels and fountains which served to irrigate the terraces, nearby courtyards and bordering areas. It is rarely visited by tourists because it is difficult to reach, but it is worthwhile to stop along the road and go up the peak to enjoy the scenery and become familiar with one of the finest examples of Incan architectural construction associated with hydraulic systems.

View from the road which leads to the Tipón ruins.

Archaeological ruins in Pikillaqta.

Sacsayhuaman or Fortress.

Sacsayhuaman.

The Sacsayhuaman or Fortress

In the mountainous region to the north of the city one can admire the ruins of the former Fortress, or Sacsayhuaman. The buildings occupy an extremely vast area, but what is most noteworthy are the three stone walls which suggest the appearance of a fortress. This extensive area also displays other elements of interest. There are figures made of stones and rocks, entrances which lead to underground tunnels or *chincanas*, amphitheaters, and buildings where rituals were performed, probably related to the water cult. The area undoubtedly played an important role in the Incan rituals and, in general, during the pre-Hispanic period. Its monumental nature makes it difficult to determine the specific function of this area. Nevertheless, the drawings on the stones and the alignment of the walls, where enormous seats have been carved, confirm the importance of the area for the Incas and their ancestors.

In recent years, tombs have been discovered in the area which do not seem to be from the most ancient times. Archaeologists believe these corpses were buried during the period near the time when the Spaniards arrived in Cuzco, in the sixteenth century.

From Sacsayhuaman one can visit other nearby areas of interest. The nearest is Quenqo, on the hill today called Socorro. Here there are natural and carved rocks and the *Intihuatana*, which served to measure time. The drawings remind one of the irrigation channels and the rituals associated with water. Pucapucara is a bit further from here. It also has channels, aqueducts, carved stones, benches and altars where sacrifices were performed. It is possible to follow this route to Tambomachay, where three beautiful fountains nurtured by the plentiful water supply provided by the small lakes in the pampas between Cuzco and the Sacred Valley can be found.

At the end of the month of June, the annual festival of *Inti Raymi* is held in Sacsayhuaman and the Incan ritual of the cult of the Sun or *Inti* is performed. This forms part of the celebration of Cuzco Week, period in which many folkloric activities are organized by groups and schools from the city. During the performance of *Inti Raymi*, the ancient rites are not followed strictly. The Inca and his wife, *la Coya,* with their escorts, go up to the Fortress, where they sing, dance and drink to the Sun and to the Mother Earth, *Pachamama*. During the celebration of *Inti Raymi*, the people from the city and the tourists spend a pleasant day on the esplanade of Sacsayhuaman.

Sacsayhuaman.

Tarahuasi

The Incan ruins of Tarahuasi are located on the road which leads from the pampas of Anta to the Apurimac River and Abancay, along a narrow route with extraordinary scenery which leads to Nevado Salkantay. Here, in the town of Limatambo, one can find well-conserved walls and monumental buildings. In the past this area, which is extremely peaceful, was the site of large haciendas where a great deal of fruit was produced, favored by the mild climate and a plentiful water supply. At present, *kiwicha* is grown in this area, and its grain is used to make bread, biscuits and rice.

«Hacienda Margarita», with Incan walls. The stones are arranged in the form of a daisy. Tarahuasi, Limatambo.

Kiwicha, on the road to Limatambo.

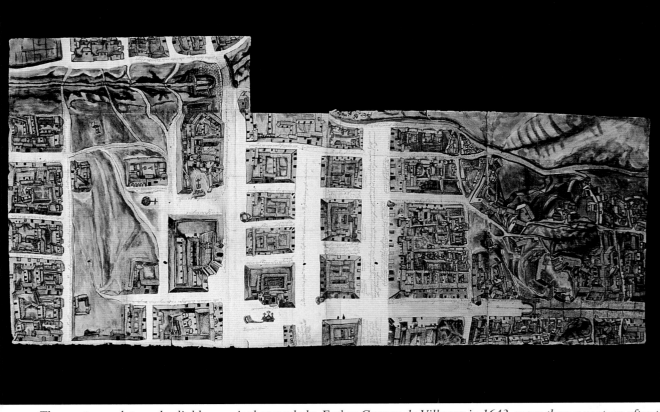

The most complete and reliable map is that made by Father Gaspar de Villagra in 1643, more than a century after the Spanish conquest of the city. The plan of the city is very similar to the present. You can see the neighborhoods and the colonial boundaries of the area of the city where the people live.

Colonial Cuzco

In 1534, the conquistador Francisco Pizarro founded the city of Cuzco in the ancient capital of the Incan empire on behalf of the emperor Charles V.

After the Spanish conquest, different building techniques, styles and materials, as well as a different perspective regarding the use of space, were employed in Cuzco. Nevertheless, the Incan traditions continued, integrating the new contributions with their own distinctive mark. In no other area of the Americas did the juxtaposition and the contrast between the indigenous and the Spanish way of life achieve more fascinating effects. Although the Spaniards cleared areas for their churches, they respected the area, the shape, the orientation and the already existing walls of the towns. Thus, today there are Incan streets which have been conserved nearly intact: Loreto, Confitería, Harinas, etc.

The colonial architecture of Cuzco has always maintained great stylistic unity, especially in the buildings constructed after the great earthquake of 1650, which razed much of the city. The churches built in the latter part of the seventeenth century are characterized by splendid facades, with solid towers and profusely decorated doors reminiscent of the arrangement and ornamentation of the Baroque altarpieces. The colonial architecture which developed in Cuzco achieved its maximum expression in the religious buildings: chapels, churches, convents and monasteries. But it was also noteworthy in the construction of civil buildings: palaces and large stately homes. At present, some of the religious and civil buildings of the colonial era have been restored and converted into museums, schools, banks and hotels.

In the period of its finest architectural splendor, Cuzco was also an important artistic center. The Mannerist style of the

Jesuit Bernardo Demócrito Bitti appeared in both Lima and Cuzco at the same time, and this was followed by other Italian Mannerist painters. After this initial European trend, colonial painting branched into different schools and circles of painters. Nevertheless, the most important development as regards painting was the Cuzco school, which spanned several periods. The end of the sixteenth century and the beginning of the seventeenth century was the period of the first Mannerist artists. Then, in the mid-seventeenth century, the Baroque period began, with artists of the stature of Basilio Santa Cruz Pumacallao and Diego Quispe Tito Inga. The following century was the period in which the popular painting of the Cuzco school flourished, with artists such as Marcos Zapata, Antonio Wilca, Basilio Pacheco and, above all, hundreds of anonymous artists painters who produced thousands of paintings in their own studios. The painting business represented a significant aspect of the colonial economy of Cuzco. During this popular stage, Neo-Mannerism was the most characteristic style, with the increased stiffness and flattening of the figures, changes in the arrangement of space, as well as brocading and gilding with gold. The final stage of the Cuzco school was represented by Andean popular painting. These works mark a definitive break with European models, producing paintings which display a syncretism which combines European elements with indigenous motifs and shapes. During this period, which took place in the early nineteenth century, Tadeo Escalante was a decisive figure.

Today one can see many examples of Cuzco painting in the Archaeological Museum; the Casa Garcilaso; the convents, monasteries and churches of the city and the Valley of Cuzco; as well as the Museo Pedro de Osma in Lima. At the same time, splendid examples of Cuzco painting can also be found in some hotels and banks, as well as other institutions, in Cuzco. During the seventeenth and eighteenth centuries there is a notable period of development in the sculptural work in Cuzco, associated above all with the decoration of the elegant churches and homes, and especially evident in the choirstalls and altarpieces made of carved wood. Thus, many of the sculptors worked as woodcarvers, or made altars and altarpieces. Diego Martínez de Oviedo, who built the altarpieces for the Church of Santa Teresa (1664) and the Church of San Sebastián (1679), is an outstanding example. He also timidly introduced the Baroque style, which would later be employed by the Indian Juan Tomás Tuyru Tupac in several churches in Cuzco, such as the Church of Almudena or the Church of San Blas.

Church of Santo Domingo constructed on the Incan ruins also known as the Temple of the Sun, or Coricancha.

Basin in the Plaza de Armas, Cuzco.

Convent and Church of Santo Domingo

The first religious order to reach Cuzco was the Order of
Santo Domingo, which entered the city in 1532. A few
years later, in 1539, Francisco Pizarro, conqueror of Peru,
decided to build the Convent or Church of Santo Domingo
in the area previously occupied by the Temple of the Sun.
Pizarro was received by fray Vicente Valverde of the
Order of Santo Domingo, a close relative of the Pizarro
family who accompanied the conquistadors and witnessed
the execution of Inca Atawallpa in Cajamarca. This church
was the most impressive building in Cuzco. The structure
makes use of the walls and the pre-Hispanic separations,
and includes beautiful arcades, a cloister with a series of
arches and the sectors set aside for the convent. In the
church and cloister one can admire canvases which portray
Christ, the Virgin and the Catholic saints.

After the most recent earthquakes, the church and the

*Cloister of the Convent of Santo Domingo and the Incan
Temple of the Sun, or Coricancha.*

They are protected and offer one of the finest examples of pre-Hispanic architecture. In the cloister, one can see a series of 31 paintings by José Espinosa (seventeenth century) which represent different moments in the life of the saint who founded the Order of Santo Domingo. Espinosa's disciples and followers distributed his work in several churches and convents of the city. The church located in the area originally designated as the Temple of the Sun is also of interest. The main altar is located in the area which faces the circular wall of the ancient temple, which includes a beautiful niche which can be admired as one gazes at the walls and gardens of the Temple of the Sun. The chapel dedicated to the brotherhood of San José de los Carpinteros, founded in 1643 by the businessman, artist, gilder and carver Juan Rodríguez Samanez, is also in the church. Many works by this master and his disciples can still be found throughout the city.

Street in the San Blas neighborhood, Cuzco.

Facade near the Plaza de Armas, Cuzco.

convent have been rebuilt and some of the pre-Hispanic separations have been restored. This allows visitors to see the area which presently serves as the cloister of the convent, where one can admire noteworthy examples of Incan architecture. Archaeologists have attributed some names and functions to these areas, many of which are hypothetical. Nevertheless, in the *Comentarios reales de los incas* (1609), the chronicler Garcilaso de la Vega provides a wide range of details regarding the different rooms in the Temple of the Sun. He maintains that there was one temple which was dedicated to the Sun and another structure for the Moon, built of gold and silver, respectively. There was also buildings which honored the Thunder and the Rainbow. Finally, according to the same chronicler, the rooms for the celebrants were located in the Temple of the Sun.

At present, some of the walls are the work of Cuzco artists.

Cathedral of Cuzco, Plaza de Armas.

The Cathedral of Cuzco

The Cathedral of Cuzco, which reflects the Renaissance or Plateresque style, is one of the finest colonial monuments. It was built in what was formerly the Huacaypata Plaza of the Incas, area in which there is no evidence of large pre-Hispanic structures. According to some sources, this was the site of the Temple of Viracocha, in the area called Quishuarcancha, which was located in what is presently the rear of the cathedral. Whatever the case, construction of the cathedral took a long time because of the magnitude of the building and variations in the terrain. Likewise, the earthquakes contributed to the difficulties in finishing construction, which did not actually occur until one century later, in the mid-seventeenth century.

The cathedral houses a vast artistic treasure. It is decorated by approximately four hundred canvases, and the images and altars include a plentiful display of gold and silver. Some paintings are the work of notable Cuzco painters such as Marcos Zapata, whose works had a significant influence which even spread to northwest Argentina. Many of his works, which date from the eighteenth century, can also be found in the churches of Cuzco or in the Church of Triunfo.

One of the most outstanding paintings of those displayed in the cathedral and in city of Cuzco is the «Master of the Earthquakes». Since the earthquake of 1650, on Holy Monday this work is crowned by the red flowers of *k'antu* and displayed in a procession. The silence and the prayers make this Catholic ritual one of the most impressive examples of Andean urban religiosity.

Since 1659 the famous bell of María Angola, associated with many popular legends, can be found in the Cathedral tower. The bell was cast near Lake Titicaca along with

Cathedral stairway. Plaza de Armas, Cuzco.

another bell called Magdalena, which collapsed in the 1650 earthquake. It weighs a ton and is made of gold, silver and bronze. They say that its echo can be heard at a distance of several kilometers.

Next to the main building there are two small churches which complement the central structure of the building and which one can enter separately. The most famous is the Church del Triunfo, which was built in 1732. This structure was meant to commemorate the victory of the Spanish in the siege of Cuzco undertaken by Manco Capac in 1536. It is said that at this time the Virgin and the Apostle James appeared and provided the Spanish residents with the strength needed to resist the attack of the rebellious Incas and help put out the fire which spread throughout the city. Since this event, the victory has been celebrated. There are several paintings which portray these events, two of which can be found in the Church of Pucyura, near Cuzco, indicated in this guide.

The Church of the Jesuits

In the history of Peruvian colonial art one can speak of several forms of Baroque: the Lima Baroque, Cuzco Baroque and Andean Baroque styles. In this case, the Church of the Jesuits is a fine example of what is referred to as Cuzco Baroque. Construction of the Church of the Jesuits began in 1578. It took more than a decade to finish the structure because of problems with the terrain, which was very swampy. The Huayna Capac and Amaru Cancha buildings, which were located in this area, were used

Tambour, dome and lantern of the Church of the Jesuits.

Night view of the Church of the Jesuits. Plaza de Armas, Cuzco.

for the construction. The design of the church followed a specific pattern. There is a single nave with two side chapels, one dedicated to the Virgin and another to an Angel. Both are separated by screens, as was the custom in Spanish cathedrals. The earthquake of 1650 damaged much of the building because of the instability of the land where it was located. The first structure had to be demolished in order to rebuild the church. A new plan also had to be designed, which is that which we can see at present. It is in the shape of a Latin cross, similar to the Church of the Jesuits in Toledo, Spain. There are two towers at the far end of the nave. The Indian chapel, which was built in the side area bordering calle Loreto, is separate from the main nave and has its own entrance and facade. The main altarpiece of the church is considered a masterpiece of Cuzco Baroque sculpture. Inside, the famous

painting portraying the marriage of Martín García de Loyola and Ñusta Beatriz is displayed. As his surname indicates, Martín was the nephew of St Ignatius of Loyola, founder of the Jesuits. He played a leading role in the capture of the Inca rebel Tupac Amaru I, and for this reason was granted several titles. His marriage to the Ñusta was not unrelated to this event, since it provided him with the goods attributed to the legacy of the Incas. The painting is from the seventeenth century, but has not been definitively attributed to a specific artist or a precise date. It recalls events of decisive political consequences. Martín and Ñusta are on one side, with St Ignatius of Loyola (1491-1556) in the center, and Ñusta Lorenza, daughter of Martín and Beatriz, and Juan, son of San Francisco Borja (1510-1572), a member of the Jesuits, on the other side. The legend of the painting states: «This marriage joins the

«Marriage of Martín de Loyola and Ñusta Beatriz»,
Anonymous. Church of the Jesuits.

«St Ignatius Preaching», by Cipriano Gutiérrez.
Church of the Jesuits   by Marcos Zapata.

Cloister of the Convent of La Merced.

Loyola and Borja families to one another and to the royal family of the Incan kings of Peru, hereby granting succession to his Excellency the Marquis of Alcañices». There is a second painting from a later date which confirms this express intention of the Jesuits: this canvas portrays the marriage of Teresa Idiáquez and Beltrán García de Loyola. The Idiáquez are related to San Francisco Javier (1506-1552), also a member of the Jesuits.

The line of succession of the Marquis of Alcañices died out at the beginning of the eighteenth century, and with it those who claimed the legacy of Sayri Tupac. Nevertheless, the battles for the hereditary rights of the line continued, and in these conflicts Tupac Amaru II, the indigenous Indian chief who led the major uprising against the exploitation of the Spaniards in 1780, also participated.

The Church of la Merced

Like the majority of the churches in Cuzco, the Church of la Merced was built during the period after the earthquake of 1650, on the site of the ruins of the first church, which was one of the oldest in Cuzco. Along with the Church of the Jesuits, the Church of la Merced is considered one of the masterpieces of the Cuzco Baroque style. The structure belongs to the Order of la Merced, which occupies the convent with the same name. It has extremely rich holdings, and claims the honor of having been one of the first churches in the city, along with the Church of Santo Domingo.

The main door of the church faces a small plaza which was formerly the city marketplace. The clergy used to take advantage of the massive gathering of the Indians in the plaza to preach to them from the facade of the church. The main cloister of the convent, which is made of finely carved stone, is one of the most beautiful works of architecture which can be found in America. The paintings displayed here portray the saints of the Order of la Merced and the rescue of the Moor prisoners, work which the order engaged in during its early stages. Some of the canvases are attributed to Cuzco masters from the seventeenth and eighteenth century: Basilio Santa Cruz and Ignacio Chacón.

The church and neighborhood of San Blas

San Blas is one of the most typical neighborhoods of the city. This was the area where many craftsmen lived before the Spanish occupation, and today many members of this trade still reside here. The characteristics of the neighborhood remind us of colonial times. Many of the Indian families which were closest to the groups which governed pre-Hispanic Cuzco lived in this area. During the colonial period they continued to perform artistic activities which created a very special atmosphere in the neighborhood, evident today in the families of craftsmen who occupy much of the square near the church. At present the architectural structures which can be found in

Church of San Blas where the famous pulpit is found.

the area are some of the most harmonious and beautiful in the city. The church, the square and the fountains have been recently restored. The Church of San Blas is simple, but inside it houses the famous seventeenth century pulpit, sculpture of high artistic value formed with a single piece of cedar wood which is considered one of the leading examples of Baroque sculpture.

From the steep, narrow streets which lead to the square and the neighborhood one can catch a glimpse of beautiful scenery in the surrounding area and in the city.

Cloister of the Convent of La Merced.

Inside the Monastery of San Antonio Abad, recently restored and converted into an elegant and comfortable hotel, the Hotel Monasterio.

Arch of Santa Clara, next to Plaza San Francisco, Cuzco.

Inner stairway in the Chapel of the Monastery of San Antonio Abad, presently the Hotel Monasterio.

«Scene with Cloth, Musicians», painting attributed to Tadeo Escalante, Capitular Hall, Museum of the Monastery of Santa Catalina.

«Portrait of an Incan lady», Anonymous, 17th century. Archaeological Museum.

‹San Sebastián, Roman Martyr», painting on panel in relief by Bernardo Demócrito Bitti. 16th century, Casa Garcilaso, Cuzco.

«The Execution of Atahuallpa», Anonymous, 18th century. Archaeological Museum, Cuzco.

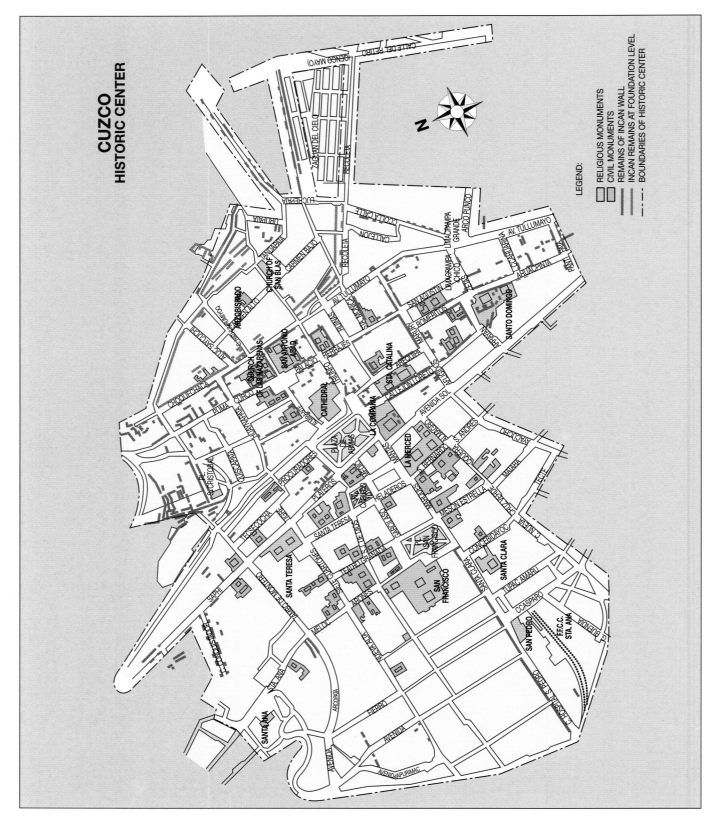

CUZCO
HISTORIC CENTER

LEGEND:

▢ RELIGIOUS MONUMENTS
▢ CIVIL MONUMENTS
REMAINS OF INCAN WALL
INCAN REMAINS AT FOUNDATION LEVEL
BOUNDARIES OF HISTORIC CENTER

Bell of the Church of Oropesa.

Churches and colonial chapels in the Cuzco Valley (See Route 1)

Oropesa and its church

South of the city, scattered throughout the valley along the road which leads from Sicuani to Lake Titicaca, there are churches of great artistic interest. Most of these are from the seventeenth century or were begun in the late sixteenth or early seventeenth century. They display many fine examples of paintings by Cuzco artists, some of them anonymous. For those interested in mural painting, a visit to these churches is highly recommended.

The Church of Oropesa is found at the beginning of a spectacular route described in the Appendix. The town of Oropesa -associated with the ancient properties of the Marquis of Oropesa in Toledo, Spain- is known in the region for its bread, and is rarely visited by tourists. Near the town, not far from Urcos, one can visit the splendid Incan ruins at Tipón.
The architectural features of the Church of Oropesa are similar to those of other churches in the region constructed in rural surroundings. It has a facade with a noteworthy balcony, also referred to as the «open chapel». These balconies were often used to preach to the masses which gathered in the plaza. The mural painting which can be

Lower choirstall of the Church of Oropesa with mural painting from the 17th century in the arcades.

Main altarpiece, 18th century. Church of Oropesa.

found in the church conserves archaisms and belongs to the oldest period of Cuzco painting, from the 1580's up to 1630. There are other paintings in the church from later periods, including the splendid canvases from the late seventeenth century displayed in the Chapel of Nazareno.

Andahuaylillas and its church

The Church of Andahuaylillas, which was built in the seventeenth century, is referred to as the «Sixtine Chapel» of Peru. It includes a single nave with an outer balcony used to preach to the public gathered in the plaza. The Mudejar style roof of the main chapel is especially noteworthy. Master Luis de Riaño was commissioned for the seventeenth century paintings. He is also responsible for other figures, including those portraying the «Road to Glory» and the «Road to Hell». The Christian soul walks towards the city of God. Riaño also painted the entrance to the baptistery, where one can find phrases referring to baptism in Puqina, a language which was rarely used and is presently extinct.

Other works by the Lima painter Luis de Riaño can also be seen in the church. These paintings would not have been possible without the presence of an exceptional figure in these works: the priest Juan Pérez de Bocanegra, who was a notable expert in Quechua. Bocanegra's works in Quechua were employed throughout the entire colony to spread the Catholic faith in the Andes and teach the Catholic catechism. In the baptismal chapel, where one can find Riaño's «The Baptism of Christ», there is a quote in Latin from 1626 referring to Riaño and to the aforementioned priest. The paintings which decorate the chapel next to the sacristy are also the work of Riaño. The main figure portrays the Ascension of Christ, and includes images of female saints and the apostles. One may also observe the work of Riaño in the choirstalls, where some noteworthy engravings have been made in the organ wood. The instruments which the angels play were undoubtedly those used in the early seventeenth century in the Catholic liturgical rites.

«Santa Cecilia with a Billet», mural painting by Luis de Riaño. 17th century, Church of Andahuaylillas.

Children of Oropesa.

Inside of the Church of Andahuaylillas.

Pentalingue Door painted by Luis de Riaño.
17th century, Church of Andahuaylillas.

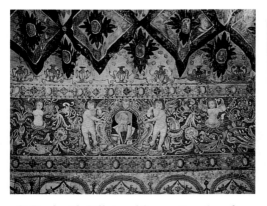

«St Paul with Billet and Supporting Angels»,
by Luis de Riaño. 17th century, Church of
Andahuaylillas.

«The Road to Heaven» by Luis de Riaño. Mural painting from 17th century, Church of Andahuaylillas.

Facade of the Church of Andahuaylillas.

Round arch, 18th century. House in the Plaza de Armas, Huaro.

Huaro and its church

In the small church in the town of Huaro one can find a series of paintings which resemble those found in the nearby Church of Andahuaylillas, some of them by Cuzco masters such as Martín Torres and Luis Riaño. The most noteworthy of these are attributed to the mestizo painter Tadeo Escalante, who was from Acomayo. The paintings by Escalante displayed in Huaro are dated in 1802. There are five groups of paintings in which St John the Baptist, patron saint of the town, is the main figure. The Popes, several saints and the Virtues, a theme often associated with this artist, are also portrayed. The most notable of these are the paintings located at the entrance to the church. Three lovers are dining when, suddenly, they are visited by Death. Christ rings a bell next to a tree to announce the end and the Virgin pleads for mercy for the diners. The Devil causes the tree to fall. Escalante also painted the scenes portrayed in «Death in the House of a Rich Man and Death in the House of a Poor Man». Death surprises the rich man while he is eating; in the house of the poor man, on the other hand, all appears to be peaceful and calm. One of the most noteworthy murals is that which portrays Hell, and is divided into two parts by a poem which says:

Ay de mi que ardiendo quedo	Oh, I am burning
Ay que pude y no puedo	Oh, I could but now Ican't
Ay que siempre he de arder	Oh, I must always burn
Ay que a Dios nunca he de ver.	Oh, I shall never see God.

«Death in the House of the Rich Man, Death in the House of a Poor Man», by Tadeo Escalante, 1802, Huaro.

Main Altar and coffered ceiling from the Church of San Juan de Huaro.

Fragment of «The Final Moments of Man, Death», by Tadeo Escalante, 1802, Huaro.

Fragment of «Final Judgement», by Tadeo Escalante, 1802, Huaro.

Fragment of «Hell», by Tadeo Escalante, 1802, Huaro.

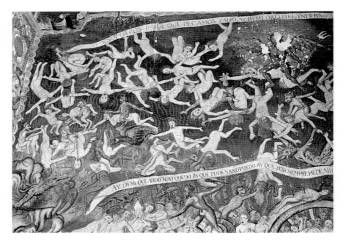

Choir, retrochoir with organ and mural painting. «Crowning of the Virgin by the Trinity», by Tadeo Escalante, Church of San Juan de Huaro.

The Chapel of Kaninkunqa

The Chapel of Kaninkunqa is not well-known among tourists or other people; nevertheless, it is worth a visit. This chapel is a small jewel which includes many of the characteristics of the mural paintings found in the churches of the region, especially the nearby Church of Andahuaylillas. It is located on a small hill not far from the city of Urcos, next to the small lake known popularly as Urcos lake. According to legend, the golden chain of Inca Huayna Capac, father of Atawallpa and Huascar, is hidden on the bed of the lake, which is bottomless and impossible to reach.

The entire inside of the chapel has been adorned with mural paintings which resemble the seventeenth century works found in nearby churches. The style of these images is more Baroque than Andahuaylillas, and the scenery is rural, including plants, flowers and small birds.

Checacupe and its church

The recently restored Church of Checaupe, which is not as well-known as the churches of Huaro and Andahuaylillas, has splendid seventeenth century paintings and carvings which are some of the finest samples of works of this type found in the churches of the region. There is a wooden «Last Supper» which historians consider one of the oldest of the South Andes. It is worth visiting this church. The comparison with Huaro and Andahuaylillas provides the visitor with a fairly good idea of the seventeenth century artistic and religious activity in the Cuzco region.

The Church of Checacupe is also an excellent example of the Cuzco mural painting which is so highly admired by those interested in this subject and so plentiful in the region. The paintings are some of the oldest in the Cuzco region, and include several noteworthy figures including the twelve apostles, San Lorenzo, and San Sebastián, as well as a series dedicated to the life of Jesus: «Childhood», «The Flight to Egypt», «The Adoration of the Magi». The scenes display a notable Flemish influence.

Anonymous Cuzco painting. 17th century, Church of Checacupe.

«Adoration of the Child by the Magi», Anonymous Cuzco painting. 17th century, Church of Checacupe.

Coffered ceiling in the presbytery, Church of Checacupe.

Shop which sells candles.

Cuzco art and tradition

Craftsmen

Since the initial contacts between the Spaniards and the people of the Andes, mutual forms of learning and work have been developed. In many cases pre-Hispanic techniques and forms of expression were conserved. At other times, the people adapted to European techniques. This dialogue has brought about the variety of artistic expressions which presently characterizes Cuzco craftsmanship: a wide range of textile and ceramic products, wood work, clay figures, wooden sculptures, paintings, masks, wax candles, etc. Many of these are produced for the city market, but often the products are also sold locally, especially during the periods when the feast days of patron saints are celebrated and clothing is needed for the dancers, masks, candles, embroidered standards, etc. The construction of churches, convents and palaces also required a wide range of craftsmen, and their work is especially evident in the marvelous altarpieces, pulpits, etc. Many of the balconies, platforms and doorways of the city of Cuzco are also a clear testimony of the artistic richness of Cuzco craftsmen since ancient times, tradition which has been conserved in some families of craftsmen.

Many cities of the Andes conserve handicrafts made by these craftsmen.

In the city of Cuzco, the San Blas neighborhood is the area where the largest number of craftsmen have lived since pre-Hispanic times. Some families of craftsmen have created their own of clay figures, now recognized throughout the world. The Mérida and the Mendivil families are some of the most outstanding of these. The former, with their clay sculptures with distressed expressions, and the latter, with their sculptures with elongated necks which portray the Three Kings, angels, pregnant virgins, etc. There are also many anonymous

Miguel Angel León, wood carver and sculptor, Cuzco.

«Women Spinning», by the sculptor Mérida, San Blas neighborhood.

«Man Drinking Beer», by the sculptor Mérida, San Blas neighborhood.

craftsmen who work on the reproduction of paintings from the so-called Cuzco colonial school. Some of these are able to achieve accurate reproductions of these paintings or, in many cases, they have created their own versions based on prior paintings.

The works made of silver and gold also play an important role in Cuzco craftsmanship, which reproduces traditional designs from the pre-Hispanic as well as the colonial period, often combined with modern designs. One of the most original jewelers of Cuzco is Carlos «Chaquira»,

Pregnant Virgin and sculptress, Georgina Dueñas, widow of Mendivil, Mendivil studio-museum, Plaza San Blas, Cuzco.

Works by Mendivil, Mendivil studio-museum, Plaza San Blas, Cuzco.

Jewels by Carlos «Chaquira», jeweler in Calle Triunfo, Cuzco.

who has created his own style by designing pieces of silver which link ancient tradition and modernity with great sensitivity and include symbols often found in the ceramics, fabrics, etc. from the pre-Hispanic period. These are often combined with a wide variety of stones: the most notable of these are the *chaquiras*. In the streets near the Plaza de Armas and in the area of the San Blas neighborhood, as well as in some hotels, there are many places where one can purchase jewels and articles made of silver.

At present Cuzco is also an important center for the manufacture of imitation jewelry (earrings and necklaces) made of *alpaca*, and often joined with Brazilian stones. In these workshops pieces are produced not only for sale in Cuzco, but also for export to foreign countries. For this reason, these pieces are often seen in the handicraft street markets of many European cities.

Out of all the thousands of pieces displayed in the shops and markets it is not always easy to distinguish between the typical craftsmanship of Cuzco and work from other Peruvian or Andean regions, in part because in recent years Cuzco craftsmen produce handicrafts typical of other regions, for example, the well-known altarpieces or tapestries of Ayacucho.

Craftswomen in the 1st May Demonstration, Plaza de Armas, Cuzco.

Cuzco schoolchildren.

MAP OF THE CUZCO REGION

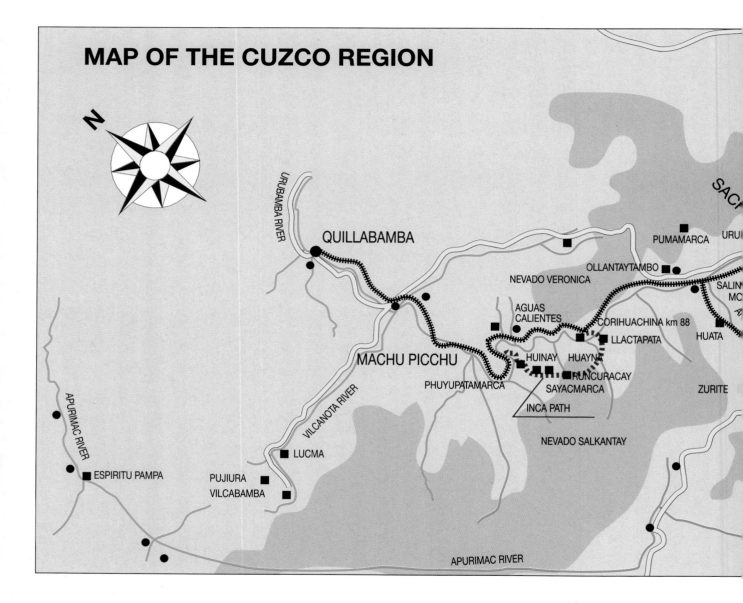

N

URUBAMBA RIVER

QUILLABAMBA

SAC

PUMAMARCA   URU

OLLANTAYTAMBO

NEVADO VERONICA

SALIN
MC
A

AGUAS
CALIENTES

CORIHUACHINA km 88

LLACTAPATA

HUATA

MACHU PICCHU

HUINAY   HUAYNA

PHUYUPATAMARCA

RUNCURACAY

SAYACMARCA

ZURITE

INCA PATH

VILCANOTA RIVER

NEVADO SALKANTAY

APURIMAC RIVER

LUCMA

ESPIRITU PAMPA

PUJIURA

VILCABAMBA

APURIMAC RIVER

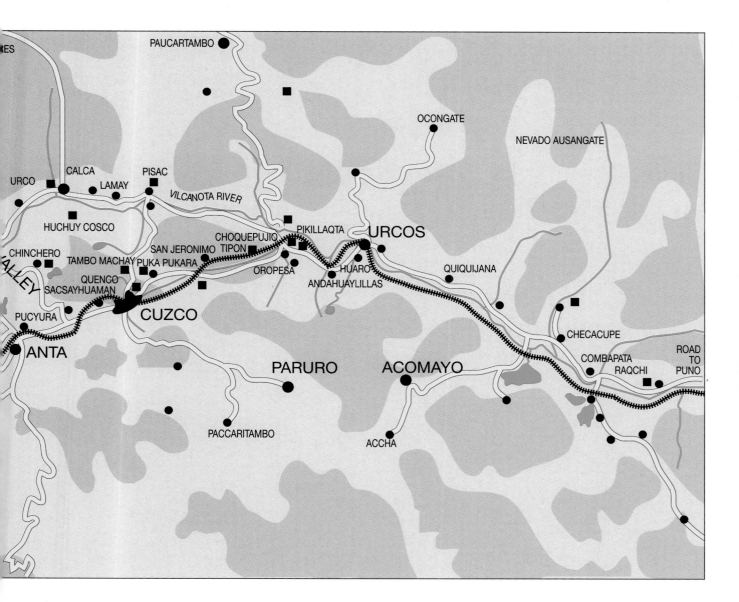

PAUCARTAMBO

OCONGATE

NEVADO AUSANGATE

CALCA
URCO
LAMAY
PISAC
VILCANOTA RIVER

HUCHUY COSCO

PIKILLAQTA
URCOS

CHINCHERO
CHOQUEPUJIO
SAN JERONIMO
TIPON

TAMBO MACHAY
PUKA PUKARA
OROPESA
HUARO
QUIQUIJANA

QUENCO
SACSAYHUAMAN
ANDAHUAYLILLAS

PUCYURA

CUZCO
CHECACUPE

ANTA

ROAD
TO
PUNO

PARURO
ACOMAYO
COMBAPATA
RAQCHI

PACCARITAMBO
ACCHA

Unku Inca, Museo de América, Madrid.

Alpacas.

Andean fabrics

If there is any form of art which can be considered deeply rooted in the Andean world it is that associated with fabrics. Today on the streets of Cuzco, as well as in other regions of the Andes, one can often see native women with a *pushka* (distaff) hanging from their waist so that they can spin as they walk, go on a visit or rest. During the pre-Hispanic period the production of fabrics was already a source of inspiration and one of the finest forms of art and technology. Through fabrics, as well as ceramics, Andean society - inspired by the natural world in their surroundings, astronomical phenomenon, customs, history, etc. -expressed their longings, their aspirations, their feelings, as well as their sense of rebellion and protest. The wide range of phases involved in the production of a fabric -which can briefly be summarized as obtaining the wool, then washing, spinning, dyeing, warping and finishing- generated an entire series of activities of economic, social and ritual nature in the pre-

Woman spinning.

Seller of wool in the Pisac Sunday market.

Spinner in the Chinchero Sunday handicraft market.

Hispanic world which served as a cohesive element for Andean society as a whole. The instruments used in the art of making fabrics were especially rudimentary and were manufactured by the weavers themselves, in contrast with the sophistication of the fabrics they produced.

Unlike the cultures which lived along the coast and used cotton, since pre-Incan times the fiber which has been most widely used in the mountainous regions is the wool from *llamas, alpacas* and *vicuñas*.

The dyeing performed in the Andes was based on extracting not only the basic colors, but an infinite number of shades, from a relatively small range of sources such as plants, bark, trees, flowers, etc. The colors did not fade nor become discolored because the proper techniques were used to apply the wide range of colors used in dyeing. The contrasting combinations of colors were employed to portray a full range of motifs on the fabrics including simple geometric figures as well as phytological, zoomorphic and anthromorphic figures, or images portraying symbols, customs and historical events. Each town had its own symbols and its own clothing. Thus the clothes one wore were a sign of identity and indicated the origins of the persons, their civil status, etc. After the conquest, the Spaniards introduced the textile techniques and instruments dominant in Europe in the Andes. They also brought sheep, and thus included a new fiber: lamb's wool. All of this occurred in conjunction with the use of new materials for dyeing which were imported from other regions of America: indigo, *palo brasil* and *palo campeche*. With all of these innovations the Spanish colonizers created *obrajes* (centers of textile production) in many areas of the Andes. These were operated by a native labor force which became one of the basic pillars of the colonial system, especially in those areas such as Cuzco which lacked minerals. The production performed in the *obrajes* specialized in the manufacture of simple lamb's wool fabrics of a single color, made especially to supply the mining centers, the agricultural workers in the *haciendas* (estate lands) of Cuzco, native consumption, etc. In this respect, Cuzco became a key center of colonial textile

Spinner on Taquile Island. Lake Titicaca, Puno.

Seller of aniline dyes in the Pisac Sunday market.

Seller of tapestries in one of the floating islands of los Uros, Lake Titicaca, Puno.

Clothing from Ocongate.

Peasant woman from the province of Canchis.

Doña Pascuala, handicraft shop in the city of Cuzco.

Dancing children from Pumamarca and Patacancha.

Knapsacks, Cuzco craftsmanship.

production and the fabrics produced in many of its *obrajes* were used to provide supplies primarily for the markets of Cuzco and the mining centers of Upper Peru (today Bolivia). The textile production organized by the Spaniards in the *obrajes* did not fully meet the demand for a whole series of high quality fabrics (wool, silk, velvet and taffeta cloths, etc.) consumed by the Spanish and criollo population so that Cuzco, like the other regions in the viceroyalty of Peru, became a major consumer of fabrics imported from Europe. Nevertheless, neither the fabrics produced in the *obrajes* of Cuzco nor those imported from Europe were able to eliminate the rich tradition of pre-Hispanic fabrics. In their homes the native population continued to produce their clothing, or at least part of it, for self-consumption, or to supply the local markets and fairs in the surrounding areas.

In the final third of the sixteenth century the Viceroy Toledo prohibited Incan clothing, and declared that Spanish clothing must be worn. This did not actually lead to the replacement of one form of clothing by another, but rather the combination of both. In spite of foreign opposition, the natives were able to conserve many of their Incan traditions and expressions. They complied with the requirement demanding they wear Spanish clothing, but did so by gradually combining it with their own clothing. Thus,

Spanish clothing became a native form of dress, and gave rise to the vast variety and range of colors which one can observe today in the Department of Cuzco. The variety of clothing worn in the different regions can still be counted in the hundreds, even within the same town. The blankets or *llicllas* from Chinchero, Ollantaytambo, and Pitumarca are known in the region. The *ponchos* are also an example of the textile traditions in the different towns of Cuzco. In some towns, red predominates, in others black and white are the colors worn most frequently. The *ponchos* from Ollantaytambo are also used widely: they include a wide variety of figures, some of which portray historic scenes such as the uprising led by Tupac Amaru II.

At present fabrics are still produced with traditional techniques and fibers, but lamb and synthetic wool are gradually being used more frequently instead of *alpaca* or *vicuña* wool. As regards traditional dyeing techniques, aniline dyes have gradually been replaced by natural dyes. One of the major problems of the Andean regions which are traditionally producers of *alpaca* wool is that, since the nineteenth century, much of their production has been exported in order to meet the demand for this fiber on the European markets, especially the English textile fabrics. Nevertheless, in Cuzco and in the local markets such as Pisac and Chinchero, or in the handicraft shops and markets in the city, one can still find relatively old examples of the fine traditional *alpaca* fabrics, or good recent imitations of them.

In the past twenty years, thousands and thousands of old fabrics have been reused and cut to make vests, jackets, knapsacks or simply to complement leather bags. In the large cities of Europe or the United States one often sees people, especially young people, dressed with traditional Andean fabrics. There are some shops in Cuzco and Lima where one can also buy *alpaca* jerseys (*chompas*) of the highest quality made with modern designs.

A visit to the Archaeological Museum of the city to view

Spinner on Taquile Island, Lake Titicaca, Puno.

Seller of tapestries, Island of los Uros, Lake Titicaca, Puno.

Gustavo León, musician from the Cuzco group «Expresión» playing a pachaqchaki with 20 strings.

Gustavo León playing a ceramic manchaypuitu and a bone quena (Indian flute).

Andean musical instruments.

the splendid pre-Hispanic textiles is strongly recommended. Unfortunately, the sample is not very complete, but that which is displayed gives an approximate idea of Andean textile production. For those who want to become more familiar with Andean textiles, a visit to the Museo Amano in Lima is also worthwhile. Here one can find a lovely collection of textiles and explanatory materials which have been chosen with excellent criteria and describe techniques and styles. In the Museo del Oro, in Lima, and the Museo de América, in Madrid, some of the most highly valued fine pre-Hispanic textiles have also been conserved. The example shown in this guide is from the latter institution.

Andean music

Many instruments were introduced in the Andes with the arrival of the Spaniards. Nevertheless, the glass figures and other archaeological pieces indicate that during the pre-Hispanic periods there was also a wide variety of instruments. Throughout the colonial period, Andean and Spanish music and dances created original forms which spread throughout the Andes. At present the violin, the harp and the different instruments which are forms or variations of string instruments from the Spanish peninsula, such as the guitar or *charango*, are extremely well-known throughout the Andean area. Some of these, such as the *charango*, also have local variations. There are a wide variety of flutes made of bamboo cane which, along with the *zampoñas* (reed flutes), are also known as *antara* or *siku*. They make a deep, elegant sound associated with intense sensations charged with spirituality and mystery. The influence of noteworthy instruments such as *trombones*, trumpets, bass drums and other percussion instruments is also noteworthy. Often musical groups were formed as a result of the military experience of the performers, who continued to play their instruments to provide entertainment for local celebrations when they later returned to their home towns. The Bolivian groups which sprung up in the Cuzco region have led to more and more instruments and instrumental groups. The carnaval dances are also very interesting and have had an important influence in the Lake Titicaca region as well as in Oruro, Bolivia, where the so-called *Diabladas* (Devil's carnaval) are celebrated.

Grains of corn served as «piqueo» or light snacks.

Andean cuisine

Peruvian cuisine is extremely rich and varied. The Cuzco region offers us products, dishes and tastes which are completely different from those found on the Peruvian coast. The main foods used for cooking in the Cuzco area are potatoes, corn and chili pepper. A wide variety of potatoes of all tastes, shapes and colors can be found in the region. It is calculated that there are over 600 varieties of potatoes. This is a food which is truly Andean and was used in rituals during the pre-Hispanic era. The *chuños*, for example, are dehydrated potatoes which were discovered in the Incan tombs. Even today, the potato plays an important role in the culinary tradition, not only of Cuzco, but also of the Andes. This is the reason why most of the dishes prepared in Cuzco are prepared with potatoes.

A similar phenomenon occurs with corn. Like potatoes,

Baked guinea pig, chili pepper souffle, tamal, salad and browned potatoes. Traditional Cuzco cuisine.

there are also a wide range of varieties, and the corn produced in this region has the distinctive characteristic of producing a very large grain. It is used in many dishes. Delicious corn tamales are made with corn, or it can also be eaten as a *piqueo* (light snack), along with rich, tasty chili sauces.

One of the traditional Andean dishes is *cuy* (baked guinea pig). The way the guinea pig is placed on the plate and the shape of the animal may intimidate the diner. But in fact the meat is very tender and tasty. Along with the typical tamales and the famous Cuzco style filled green bell peppers, they are especially recommendable with a good glass of *Tacama Gran Reserva* or *Etiqueta Negra* Peruvian wine, which are equivalent to Chilean and European wines.

Virgin of Carmen inside the Church of Paucartambo

Los Capac Negro, feast of the Virgin of Carmen in Paucartambo.

Religious feast days

<u>Virgin of Carmen in Paucartambo</u>

Señores Caporales vamos entrando
a saludarla la Patrona
a saludarla la Señora

Hemos venido, hemos llegado
a conocerla a la Mamita
a adorarla a la Señora

La Virgen del Carmen
nos ha llamado para venerarla
para adorarla

Somos dichosos, somos alegres
de conocerla a la Patrona
de arrodillarnos ante la Virgen

Señores Caporales míos, que dicen pues
de este día, que hemos llegado,
de haber llegado a este pueblo.

Morenito chiquito, no hay que llorar
aunque vengan trabajos, no hay que llorar,
la Virgen del Carmen nos dará vida.

Lima y Potosí, todo he andado solo
a esta tierra nunca he pisado.

Vamos bailando, vamos cantando,
de haber llegado a este día,
de haber llegado a este pueblo.

«Entrance», *Negro songs,* 1920 version

The «China Majeña» of Los Majeños, feast of the Virgin of Carmen in Paucartambo.

Los Majeños, feast of the Virgin of Carmen in Paucartambo.

The contradanse, feast of the Virgin of Carmen in Paucartambo.

Incan chullpas on the road to Paucartambo. →

Bridge of Charles III in the town of Paucartambo. →

Las Waqa Waqa, feast of the Virgin of Carmen in Paucartambo.

In pre-Hispanic times, the town of Paucartambo was an important center on the trade route between the jungle and Cuzco. At the end of the eighteenth century, this region was important because of the production of coca and fabrics and during this period the town became an important administrative center. The Spanish crown ordered the construction of a new bridge not far from here, referred to as the Bridge of Charles III, which was larger and more solid than the others previously in the area. The local coca merchants and the authorities moved so as to live near the bridge which today marks the boundary of the town of Paucartambo. Thereafter, craftsmen, merchants and administrative personnel began to move to the area, and these later formed a new social group of *mestizos* which gradually became differentiated from the other peasant groups which continued to live in the old town and to celebrate the cult of the Virgin of Rosario. There are many versions of the origin of the feast day of the Virgin of Carmen in Paucartambo. Initially it was the Spaniards who introduced the practice of paying respect to this Virgin in all of the towns of the colony. For this reason, feasts were celebrated throughout America. In the town it is said that in the sixteenth century two Virgins arrived in southern Peru from Spain, one of them for the town of Puno and another for the town of Paucartambo. Some claimed that the most beautiful Virgin

historical events, which are traditionally staged in several scenes. Each group recreates moments and events which are interpreted as mythical cycles. For example, the *qulla* are the residents of the Lake Titicaca region who came to trade products in the Cuzco region; the *ch'unchus* or savages are the guardians of the Virgin, who are highly respected by the faithful and by the Virgin herself; the blacks are the slaves during colonial times; the *majeños* represent the alcohol merchants; the enemies or *auqa* from Chile take us back to the famous war of the Pacific which occurred between 1879 and 1883. The group of devils is the only one which reminds us of the religious nature of the feast: these play a rather special role. With the image of the devil, the Virgin demonstrates the supernatural forces of the celebration.

The complexity, the musical symbols, the costumes, the dances and the symbiosis between actor and spectator are the reasons why the feast of Paucartambo attracts not only the neighboring towns, but also many tourists.

During the first days of the feast many tourists take advantage of their stay in Paucartambo to visit Tres Cruces, where they can admire the horizon of the Amazon and the phenomenon of the «sun dance» at sunrise.

Church of Paucartambo. Procession of the Virgin of Carmen.

«Los Danzaq», Feast of the Virgin of Carmen in Paucartambo.

remained in Paucartambo. This caused a conflict between the two towns and the residents of Puno tried to steal her. Many times, in the Andean religious feasts, there is a sense of competition with other feast days. In this case the lovely clothing, as well as the organization and discipline of the dancers, has made the feast day of Paucartambo one of the most important of the region and it has become a model for nearby towns.

Presently there are 15 groups which participate in the feast, which is celebrated each year from July 15-19. The celebration held in the town includes a recreation of

Capac Qolla dancers and llama during the feast of the Virgin of Carmen in Paucartambo.

Qollacha Dance during the feast of the Virgin of Carmen in Paucartambo

Seller of roast meat, Paucartambo.

Sellers of sugar cane, Paucartambo.

Corn chicha.

Feast of Inti Raymi, Sacsayhuaman, Cuzco.

The *Inti Raymi*

Cuzco Week is traditionally held around 24 June, period during which the Incan feast known as *Inti Raymi* is also celebrated. According to ancient chroniclers, these celebrations were linked to the harvest and provided the opportunity for the Incas to express their appreciation to their gods -the Sun, the Moon, the Thunder, Huanacauri and the Mother Earth- for the products which ensured the sustenance of the population, singing and dancing and consuming the sacred *chicha* of the corn. The *Inti Raymi* ceremonies are performed in several towns designated for this purpose, but the most important ritual event is the beginning of the harvest, when the youth chosen for military or political activities go to the Sausero place to collect the corn. This area is located quite near the Temple of the Sun or Coricancha, in what is today the Plaza de Limacpampa Grande.

Today the staging of *Inti Raymi* does not provide an accurate image of what it was in Incan times. Nevertheless, the local public and the tourists go up to Sacsayhuaman Park to admire the performances and dances and enjoy a day of leisure, admiring the beautiful scenery of the city and the valley which can be seen from this region.

Carriers of San Sebastián in the feast of Corpus Christi, Cuzco.

San Sebastián. Corpus Christi procession, Cuzco.

Corpus Christi

Since early colonial times, the feast of Corpus Christi has been celebrated throughout the Andes. This feast, which is one of the most widespread in America, began in the Middle Ages. It provides the occasion for faithful Catholics to be united around the Eucharist. In Cuzco, the festivities last a week and are attended by many visitors from the local region as well as foreigners. During the celebrations most of the sacred images which are normally displayed in the churches of the city, or the churches of San Sebastián and San Jerónimo, are joined together in the Cathedral. Each image is accompanied by the members of the brotherhood dedicated to this figure in their respective parishes. The most important event of the feast is the moment when all of the faithful, the musicians and the saints take part in the procession around the Plaza de Armas. Some of the members of the brotherhood wear special clothing or carry elegant wax candles, embroidered images and standards. Altars such as those traditionally used in Spain and introduced in America -with images of the saints and the mirrors which so fascinated the Indians in the colony- are set up in the corners of the plaza. During the feast of Corpus Christi, a fair used to be held in the city at the same time to sell products from the valley. At present, the large number of tourists makes it difficult to conduct such an event, but there are still some tables which are prepared to offer typical foods such as the famous baked guinea pig, or cold, spicy *chiriuchu*, best when accompanied by Cuzco beer.

San Cristóbal, Corpus Christi procession, Cuzco.

Virgin of Dolorosa, Good Friday procession as it passes through the streets of Cuzco.

Virgin of Almudena, Cuzco.

Feast of Qoylllor Rit'i.

Feast of Qoyllor Rit'i.

The pilgrimage to Qoyllor Rit'i

In recent years, Qoyllor Rit'i has attracted thousands of pilgrims and visitors who gather in this town to celebrate the feast of the *Señor de Ocongate* (Lord of Ocongate). The most noteworthy aspect of the celebration is its setting. Ocongate, which is located at over 4,000 meters, is associated with the story of the appearance of the Christ Child or Emmanuel to a young shepherd, *Marianito*. The Christ Child appeared in the form of Christ on the crucifix, reason for the image displayed here. A chapel was built in Ocongate where since the eighteenth century thousands of faithful have gathered in the city of Cuzco to celebrate the feast of Corpus Christi. The local communities participate actively in the pilgrimage, although some of them are from faraway regions. During the days in which the feast is celebrated many communities sing and dance with the accompaniment of their traditional musicians. The peasants from the Q'eros region are especially noteworthy, with their typical clothing and traditional songs. In recent years pilgrims from Bolivia have also taken part in the celebration, along with their musicians and dancers. Besides the religious aspect -the memory of the appearance of the Lord-, there is also a pilgrimage to the snowcapped peak located at over 5,000 meters. The peasants make the pilgrimage to the mountaintop, where they cut pieces of ice and carry them back to Ocongate. The temperatures are quite low, and those who make the pilgrimage risk their lives in these frozen peaks.

Pucyura: «The Death of the Inca»

To the north of Cuzco, not far from the city, one can find the town of Pucyura. The patron saint of this area is San Salvador, or *Q'uchuy*, and his feast day is celebrated on August 6. In the church, which otherwise has been neglected, some canvases have been conserved. Two of these represent scenes from the siege of Cuzco by Manco II, portrayed in a style which suggests they are from the eighteenth century.

Pilgrims in the feast of Qoyllor Rit'i, Nevado Ausangate.

Incas during the feast of Q'uchuy in Pucyura.

Feast of Q'uchuy in Pucyura.

Patrons of the feast of San Salvador or Q'uchuy in Pucyura.

Spanish and Incan children during the feast of Q'uchuy in Pucyura.

These exceptional paintings also include figures from the native elite during this period. Pucyura is also of interest for other reasons. During the feast, the townspeople perform the «Death of the Inca», a recreation of the battles between the Incas and the Spaniards which offers a likely explanation for the aforementioned canvases. From very early times these battles were recreated in the Andean towns. There is evidence from the mid-sixteenth century which suggests that during this period these scenes were already performed in Potosí, on the hill of silver. There are also testimonies indicating that these performances became more widespread over time. They are reminiscent of the recreations of the «battles between the Moors and the Christians» which were popular for centuries in Spain. The people of Pucyura have added modern elements to the performance, including scenes not related to the Spanish conquest

Markets

The tradition of trade fairs and markets began in the Andes many years ago. There are still some fairs which are celebrated each year, such as the Tio Fair, near the town of Maras, in the pampa, where the feast of the Assumption is celebrated in mid-August; the Cuzco Fair held in the city during the feast of Corpus Christi; and the *Santurantikuy* Fair, which is held on 24 December in the Plaza de Armas of Cuzco and is attended by peasant families from regions outside Cuzco, including the

southern Andes and Bolivia. The great centers of pilgrimage of the region such as the feast of the *Señor de Huanca* (Lord of Huanca) held in the town of San Salvador in September and the feast of Qoyllor Rit'i, celebrated in June and July, are also combined with these types of fairs and markets. There are usually a wide range of stands at these events which offer typical food and drink, products of the region, popular craftsmanship and ceramics or, as in the case of *Santurantikuy*, display a whole series of products often employed in Christmas nativity scenes. Along with

Carriers in the Calle de las Sietes Culebras (Street of the Seven Snakes), Cuzco.

Carriers from Chinchero.

Sellers in the Pisac market.

Children from Pisac.

Drinking juice in the San Francisco market, Cuzco.

Seller of meringue in the Pisac Sunday market.

all of these traditional products, at present the fairs are also crowded with occasional sellers who offer products manufactured in modern Peruvian or foreign factories. These annual fairs are often the only time when the peasants who live in the most isolated communities can purchase industrial or modern products.

The markets are held every Sunday in different towns of the Cuzco region. This is the day when many peasants go to church and, after mass, take advantage of the opportunity to trade, sell or purchase products. In recent years, the popularity of the Chinchero market, which is held near the parish church, has increased. But the most well-known market is the Pisac market, also held near the church, in the main square of the town. Here products from the valley and typical clothing from the Andean region are displayed and sold. Years ago in Pisac it was common to see the local residents trading their products, as in the Chinchero market. In Pisac, the celebration of the Sunday mass in the Quechua language, accompanied by traditional songs, is an important event in the day. The mass is presided over by the local authorities, dressed in their traditional clothing and with their symbols of power, including notable elements such as the *varayoq* (rod or staff of authority). For this reason, the authorities

A couple in love, Pisac.

Seller of coca leaves in the Pisac Sunday market.

are also referred to as *varayoq*. After mass, the visitors disperse throughout the valley and, taking advantage of the mild climate and the splendid scenery of the hills and the peaks, rest and have lunch in one of the many restaurants in the valley.

In the Appendix (See Route 2) some local markets which are not often visited by tourists are mentioned. In fact, in many towns the Sunday markets where products of the region are traded are held in circumstances similar to those of Chinchero and Pisac. The Sunday mass serves as the occasion to gather a large number of townspeople in the main square. In the city there are also markets where local,

Ancahuasi market.

Seller, Curahuasi.

Los Varayoqs, Chinchero.

regional and national products are sold daily. In Cuzco there is the San Pedro market, near the train station which leads to Machu Picchu; the Huanchac market, to the south of the city; the informal market held in the Avenida del Ejército; and the San Francisco market, next to the square with the same name. In the latter, there are also sellers of handicrafts located near the market which sells the usual products.

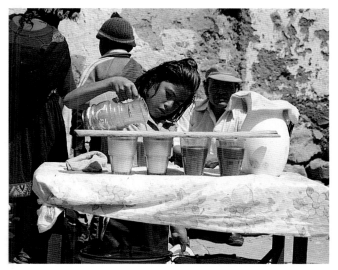

Seller of corn chicha and rosary beads, Pisac.

◁ *Handicraft market in Chinchero.*

Townspeople of Pisac.

Santirantikuy Fair, 24 December. Plaza de Armas, Cuzco.

Arch on Taquile Island.

Cattail raft and rower. Lake Titicaca, Puno. ▷

Lake Titicaca
(See Route 5)

Lake Titicaca, located in southern Cuzco on the border between Peru and Bolivia, is not in the Department of Cuzco, but we have included it in this guide because this journey is often made from the city of Cuzco.

On the islands and along the shores of Lake Titicaca, one can find a variety of archaeological sites and typical towns of the lake region. From Puno or other towns along the shores of Lake Titicaca one can travel to the Islands of the Sun and the Moon where, according to some legends, the Incas originated. Taquile Island is famous for its craft production, particularly for its beautiful textiles, and the floating islands of los Uros are inhabited by fishermen and hunters. The residents of los Uros use the cattail, a type of rush which grows in the lake, to create the conditions which ensure the islands stay afloat. The dense roots which the plants develop support the island.

Since the sixteenth century, the residents of los Uros has always been unjustly looked down upon. Today, a significant amount of people from this region live in Bolivian territory. They have developed forty floating islands on the lake. The roofs are waterproof and the houses are extremely humid because of the surrounding water. At present they speak Quechua and Aymara.

Island of los Uros. Lake Titicaca, Puno.

Women from Taquile Island. Lake Titicaca, Puno.

Attractive routes near Cuzco

The route south to Raqchi (Route 1)

On this first route two different trips are suggested. First of all, a visit to the beautiful churches located in the area. Secondly, a visit to the Incan ruins.

It is quite easy to hire a taxi or organize a tour with an agency to reach these places. Transport by bus is offered at regular intervals and is inexpensive, although less safe. It is a bit difficult to reach the Tipón ruins. One must tell the taxi driver to cross the Vilcanota River, which is not high during the tourist season (July-August). It is recommended that you take food because there are few restaurants in the area.

As for visiting churches, the Church of Andaduaylillas usually has regular visiting hours, but for some other churches you will often have to seek out the *ecónomo* (ecclesiastical administrator) of the town so that he can open the door. In this case, it is recommendable to provide a tip to facilitate entrance. There is no charge for visiting the Pikillaqta and Tipón ruins. This is not the case for the Raqchi ruins, where one can admire the pre-Incan walls associated with the mythical hero Viracocha and the colonial church, but must pay an entrance fee not included in the «tourist ticket».

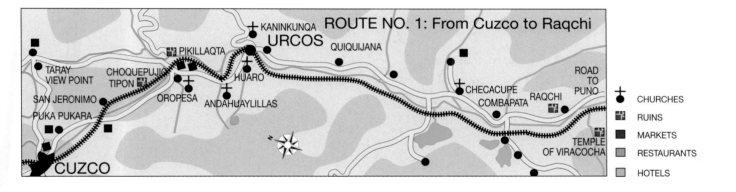

The Sacred Valley (Route 2)

This route is the most well-known and best organized by the travel agencies. It is worthwhile to plan the trip to las Salinas (the salt flats) of Maras with an agency, as this area is often not visited by tourists and agencies. In order to see all of the places mentioned we suggest that you spend a night in a hotel in Urubamba or Pisac. This trip offers a wide variety of scenery, ruins and crafts markets. On Sunday the Pisac market is an area of special interest for tourists.

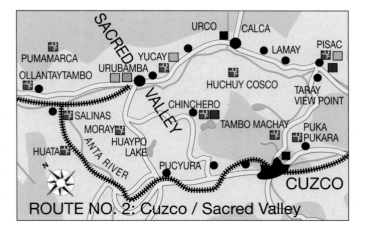

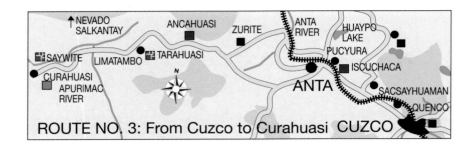

ROUTE NO. 3: From Cuzco to Curahuasi

The route northward to Curahuasi (Route 3)

This trip shall allow you to enjoy some of the most beautiful scenery of the region including the view of Nevado Salkantay, which borders the Apurimac River. This route is rarely offered by travel agencies and tourist services are nearly non-existent. We suggest visiting the traditional markets of Ancahuasi and Iscuchaka on Sunday. For this reason, it is a good idea to make the trip a day-long excursion by hiring a taxi or planning the trip with a travel agency. In Pucyura you can visit the church which has two noteworthy paintings. We also recommend having a delicious natural juice in the Iscuchaka market before continuing on to Ancahuasi, where you can see the traditional Sunday market. The road then leads us to Limatambo, where the Tarahuasi ruins and splendid Incan architecture can be found. The climate becomes hotter and the colors and vegetation are more varied and beautiful. The next area of interest is the majestic Apurimac River which shall take us to Curahuasi, town associated with anis. Not far from here is the famous carved stone of Saywite, an extraordinary work with some engravings which seem to suggest a symbolic and urban plan for the town.

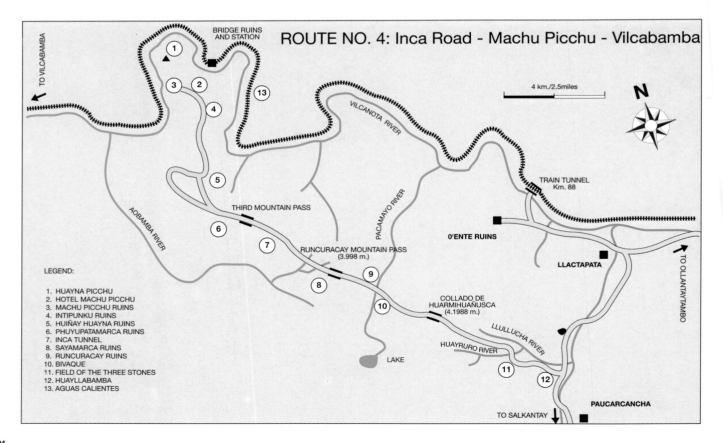

ROUTE NO. 4: Inca Road - Machu Picchu - Vilcabamba

LEGEND:

1. HUAYNA PICCHU
2. HOTEL MACHU PICCHU
3. MACHU PICCHU RUINS
4. INTIPUNKU RUINS
5. HUIÑAY HUAYNA RUINS
6. PHUYUPATAMARCA RUINS
7. INCA TUNNEL
8. SAYAMARCA RUINS
9. RUNCURACAY RUINS
10. BIVAQUE
11. FIELD OF THE THREE STONES
12. HUAYLLABAMBA
13. AGUAS CALIENTES

The Inca Path (Route 4)

The Inca Path (*El camino inca*) is very well-travelled in July and August. It is recommended that you make your visit with a travel agency and a guide who knows the region well. It is also recommendable to rest a few days when you arrive in Cuzco before taking this excursion, which requires a good level of physical fitness. The altitude sickness, or *soroche*, makes physical exercise more difficult. After arriving at the Machu Picchu ruins, it is suggested that you continue up the valley until you reach the Vilcabamba ruins, area which was the final refuge of the Incas.

The route to Lake Titicaca (Route 5)

The most recommended form of travel for this route is by plane, which takes 30 minutes from Cuzco. The flight is reasonably priced and is worthwhile, since the trip by bus is quite long (at least 11 hours), not overly safe and extremely tiring. The plane arrives in Juliaca, where there are buses awaiting the travellers which transport them to hotels in Puno. From this town you can reach the lake and, if you wish to visit the islands, there are many boats throughout the day. Since the sun is very strong in this area, travellers should take precautions against sun burn, as well as the cold during the boat trip, and the soroche. One must not forget that Lake Titicaca is at an altitude of 3,660 meters above sea level. After you have reached your destination, the beauty and the variety of the scenery which awaits you shall make you forget the small inconveniences of the trip.

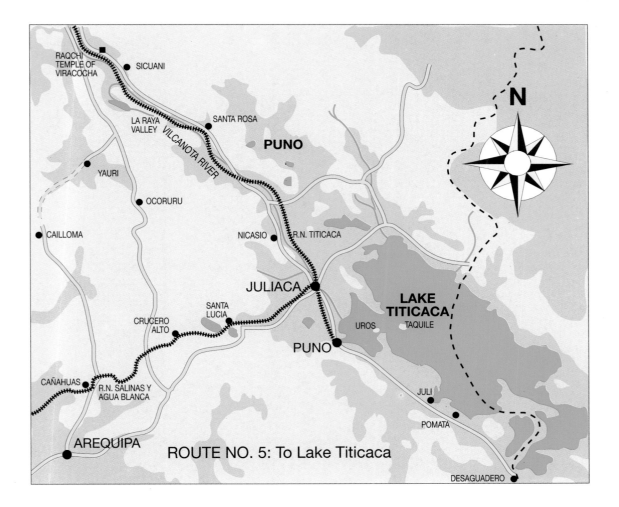

ROUTE NO. 5: To Lake Titicaca

Bibliography

Antúnez de Mayolo, Santiago E., *La nutrición en el Antiguo Perú*, Banco Central de Reserva, Lima, 1981.

Cobo, Bernabé, *Historia del Nuevo Mundo* (1653), I-II, Biblioteca de Autores Españoles, Madrid, 1964.

Escandell-Tur, Neus, *Producción y comercio de tejidos coloniales: los obrajes y chorrillos del Cusco 1570-1820*, Editorial Centro de Estudios Regionales Andinos Bartolomé de las Casas, Cuzco, 1997.

Esquivel y Navia, Diego de, *Noticias cronológicas de la gran ciudad del Cuzco*, I-II, (c.1749), Biblioteca de la Cultura Peruana, Banco Wiese, Lima, 1980.

Guamán Poma de Ayala, Felipe, *Nueva crónica y buen gobierno*, Institut d'Ethnologie, Paris, 1936.

Inca Garcilaso de la Vega, *Comentarios reales de los Incas* (1609), Banco de Crédito del Perú, Lima, 1985.

Mesa, José de y Teresa Gisbert, *Historia de la pintura cuzqueña*, I-II, Banco Wiese, Lima, 1982.

Molina, Cristóbal de, *Fábulas y mitos de los Incas (1574-1575)*, ed. Henrique Urbano, Historia 16, Madrid, 1988.

Polo de Ondegardo, *El mundo de los Incas*, ed. Laura González y Alicia Alonso, Historia-16, Madrid, 1990.

Tamayo Herrera, José, *Nuevo compendio de Historia del Perú*, Editorial Osiris, Lima, 1986.

Urbano, Enrique, comp., *Mito y simbolismo en los Andes, Centro Bartolomé de las Casas*, Cuzco, 1993.

Urbano, Enrique, *Wiracocha y Ayar. Héroes y funciones en las sociedades andinas*, Centro Bartolomé de las Casas, Cuzco, 1981.

Vidal de Milla, Delia, *La textilería indígena*, Cuzco, 1983.

Villasante Ortiz, Segundo, *Paucartambo: Provincia folklórica Mamacha Carmen*, Tomo II, Editorial León, Cuzco, s/f.

Index

Prologue	2
Pre-Hispanic Cuzco	4
Machu Picchu	11
Map of Machu Picchu	15
Sacred Valley of the Incas	17
Pre-Hispanic towns of the valley of Cuzco	25
Colonial Cuzco	29
Map of the city of Cuzco	40
Temples and colonial chapels in the Cuzco Valley	41
Cuzco art and tradition	51
Map of the Cuzco region	56-57
Religious feasts	68
Markets	81
Itineraries and maps	93

First edition printed on june 1997 by Fisa-Escudo de Oro
C/. Palaudàries, 26 - 08004 Barcelona, SPAIN
3000 copies.